PIANO FUN

BOOK TWO

by Nancy M. Poffenberger

A Simple, Self-Teaching Method

ISBN 0-938293-26-5

*PATENT PENDING

DEDICATION

To: **Beth Burtschy**
     Ginny Isgrig
     Peggy Lyon
     Barbara Young

Each one helped in a different way for **Piano Fun Book Two** to become a reality. My thanks to these very special friends!

INTRODUCTION

HAVE YOU EVER WISHED YOU COULD PLAY THE PIANO OR ORGAN? WELL, NOW YOU CAN **TEACH YOURSELF** AND MOVE AT YOUR OWN PACE.

Through **Piano Fun Book One** many people have learned the basics of piano and organ ... mainly where the different keys lie and the sound each key makes.

Others of you, with **Piano Fun Book Two,** will be trying to play the piano or organ for the first time. This book is written in a manner to enable you to play successfully without any previous piano or organ experience. If you are less than nine years of age though, it is recommended that you complete **Piano Fun Book One** before attempting this book.

Piano Fun Book Two will now take you through:

1. Naturals, Sharps, and Flats with tunes using them.

2. Fingering.

3. Three Chords-play songs with two hands now!

4. Rhythm.

5. Reading Music-play simple melodies now by reading notes.

AND SO THE FUN GOES ON............

I do not promise this book will make you a concert pianist, but I do promise, if you follow directions and practice what I suggest, that you will have a lot of fun while enjoying **instant success.**

DOs AND DON'Ts FOR KEYBOARD FUN

FOR THIS PART OF THE BOOK:

DO: *PLAY THE ORANGE AND BROWN-LETTERED NOTES WITH YOUR **RIGHT** HAND.......
PLAY BLACK-LETTERED NOTES WITH YOUR **LEFT** HAND.

*USE THE FINGER THAT IS MOST COMFORTABLE FOR YOU.

*PLAY EACH SONG USING THE RHYTHM **YOU** REMEMBER. THIS IS ONE OF THE GREATEST STRENGTHS OF THIS
TEACHING METHOD...THE RHYTHM IS BUILT-IN.

*HAVE FUN WHILE LEARNING AND PLAYING!

DON'T: *WORRY IF YOU MAKE MISTAKES AT FIRST.....THIS IS HOW **EVERYONE** LEARNS TO PLAY THE PIANO OR ORGAN.

*GO ON IN THE BOOK UNTIL YOU HAVE LEARNED THE SONG YOU ARE PLAYING. THIS BOOK BUILDS ON WHAT YOU
HAVE ALREADY LEARNED AND THERE IS NO WAY YOU CAN PLAY THE END OF THE BOOK WITHOUT LEARNING **WELL**
THE BEGINNING OF THE BOOK.

TO GET YOUR KEYBOARD READY

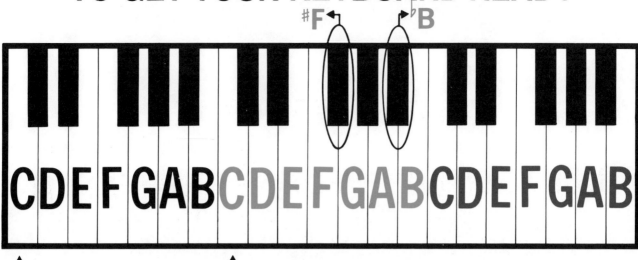

17th White Key On Piano (from left to right)

middle C on piano
— OR —
The C in the middle of your portable keyboard

PLACE TABS ON WHITE KEYS FIRST:

1. Going from left to right on your piano, count up 17 white keys. (This is on a standard piano.)

*For Organs and other keyboard instruments, find Middle C and follow above example.

2. On the 17th white key, place the black lettered tabs starting with the black "C" then the black "D" and so on as shown above.

3. After you have put on the last black "B" tab, then start with the Orange "C" and place the Orange lettered tabs on through the Orange "B" as shown above.

4. After you place the last Orange "B" tab on, follow with the Brown "C" through the Brown "B".

It will help as you proceed with this book if you will memorize this order – CDEFGABC. This is called an "Octave" (8 consecutive notes).

If you are not comfortable placing the stickers on your keyboard, you may make your own with masking tape or else use magic markers (orange, black & brown) that are _ERASABLE_.

TABS FOR THE BLACK KEYS:

In this book you will learn F Sharp and B Flat in the orange lettered notes; so we will now place these tabs on your keyboard.

1. The F Sharp tab is shown as **#F** and is placed on the black key between the Orange F and the Orange G. (See drawing above.)

2. The B flat is shown as **♭B** and is placed on the black key between the Orange A and the Orange B (See above.)

3

TABLE OF CONTENTS

FOR HE'S A JOLLY GOOD FELLOW

G E E E D E F E

FOR   HE'S   A   JOL....LY   GOOD   FEL....LOW

E D D D C D E C

FOR   HE'S   A   JOL....LY   GOOD   FEL....LOW

C E E E D E F A

FOR   HE'S   A   JOL....LY   GOOD   FEL....LOW

A G G G F D C

WHICH   NO....BODY   CAN   DE....NY.

Play all orange and brown lettered notes with your right hand; all black with your left.

OH! SUSANNA

C D E G G A G E C D

I..... CAME TO AL....A.....BA....MA WITH MY

E E D C D C D E G

BAN.....JO ON MY KNEE AND I'M GOING TO

G A G E C D E E D D C

LOUI.....SI.....AN.....A MY TRUE LO....VE FOR TO SEE

F F A A A G G E C

OH! SU....SAN.....NA, OH DON'T YOU CRY FOR

D C D E G G A G E

ME, I.....'VE COME FROM AL.....A.....BA....MA

C E E D D C

MY BAN.....JO ON MY KNEE.

Play all orange and brown lettered notes with your right hand; all black with your left.

6

AMERICA

C C D B C D

MY COUN.....TRY 'TIS OF THEE

E E FE DC DCBC

SWEET LAND OF LI.....BER.....TY ⁻ OF THEE I SING

G G GG F E

LAND WHERE MY FA.....THER DIED

F FF F E D

LAND OF THE PIL.....GRIM'S PRIDE

EFEDC E FG

FROM EV.....ER.....Y MOUN.....TAIN.....SIDE

AF E DC

LE ....T FREE.....DOM RING.

Play all orange and brown lettered notes with your right hand; all black with your left.

7

YANKEE DOODLE

C C D E C E D G C C

YAN....KEE DOO....DLE WENT TO TOWN A RID....ING

D E C B G C C D E F E

ON A PO....NY. HE STUCK A FEA....THER IN HIS

D C B G A B C C

HAT AND CALL....ED IT MA....CAR....RONI.

A B A G A B C G A

YAN....KEE DOO....DLE KEEP IT UP YAN....KEE

G F E G A B A G A

DOO....DLE DAN....DY. ALL THE LASS....ES ARE

B C A G C B D C C

SO SWEET. AS SWEET AS SU....GAR CAN....DY.

Play all orange and brown lettered notes with your right hand; all black with your left.

8

INTRODUCING NATURALS, FLATS AND SHARPS

1. What are Naturals? The four songs you have just played use all natural notes. For those of you who played Piano Fun Book One, all the notes in there were natural. There was no mention of a sharp or a flat.

2. What are sharps? Sharps are one-half step higher than the original or natural note and lie directly to the right of the white key. If you look at your keyboard, you will see that all the keys except E and B have a black key to their direct right...these black keys are called Sharps. E and B have white keys to their direct right and these will be their sharps.

3. What are flats? Flats are one-half step lower than the original or natural note and lie directly to the left of the white natural key. If you look at your keyboard you will see that all but two keys have a black flat directly to the left of them. The two that don't are C and F and those two keys use the white key to their direct left to be their flat.

The above material will mean much more to you after you become more familiar with your piano and the playing of songs so

LET'S GET ON WITH THE FUN!

INTRODUCING THE B FLAT IN THE ORANGE SECTION

A flat is the key directly to the left of the white key. In this book we will be using the black key in between the orange-lettered A and orange-lettered B on your keyboard. This black key will appear as

Now turn the page and enjoy playing the following songs with ♭**B** in them. If you have difficulty with the following songs, I suggest you practice further the preceding songs. For more songs using only naturals, I recommend **Piano Fun Book One**.

SKIP TO MY LOU

☛ **Remember: B Flat is shown as ♭B.**

A A F F A A C

LOST MY PART...NER, WHAT'LL I DO?

G G E E G G ♭B

LOST MY PART...NER WHAT'LL I DO?

A A F F A A C

LOST MY PART...NER WHAT'LL I DO?

G A ♭B A G F F

SKIP TO MY LOU, MY DAR...LING.

2nd Verse:

I'll Get Another One, Better Than you,

I'll Get Another One, Better Than you,

I'll Get Another One, Better Than You,

Skip To My Lou, My Darling.

Play all orange and brown lettered notes with your right hand; all black with your left.

HOME ON THE RANGE

☛ Remember: B Flat is shown as ♭B.

C C F G A   F   E D ♭B ♭B ♭B

OH, GIVE ME A HOME   WHERE THE BUF... FA... LO ROAM,

A ♭B C F F F E F G   C

WHERE THE DEER AND THE AN...TE...LOPE PLAY,   WHERE

C F G A F E D ♭B ♭B ♭B ♭B ♭B

SEL...DOM IS HEARD   A DIS...COUR...A...GING WORD,   AND THE

A G F E F G F C ♭B A G

SKIES ARE NOT CLOUD...Y ALL DAY.   HOME HOME ON THE

A C C F F F F E F

RANGE   WHERE THE DEER AND THE AN...TE...LOPE

G C C F G A F E D ♭B ♭B

PLAY. WHERE SEL...DOM IS HEARD A DIS...COUR...A...GING

♭B ♭B ♭B A G F E F G F

WORD,   AND THE SKIES ARE NOT CLOUD...Y ALL DAY.

Play all orange and brown lettered notes with your right hand; all black with your left.

CLEMENTINE

☛ **Remember: B Flat is shown as ♭B.**

FFF C AAAF   FACC

IN A CAV...ERN,   IN A CAN...YON,   EX...CA...VA...TING

♭BAG G A♭B♭B AGAF

FOR   A MINE,   DWELT A MIN... ER,   FOR...TY NIN...ER,

FAG C E GF

AND HIS DAUGH...TER CLEM...EN...TINE.

FFFC   AAAF

CHORUS:

OH, MY DAR...LING,   OH MY DAR...LING,

FACC♭BAG

OH MY DAR...LING CLEM...EN...TINE!

GA♭B♭B A GAF

YOU ARE LOST AND GONE   FOR...EV...ER,

F A GCE GF

DREAD...FUL SOR...RY, CLEM...EN...TINE!

Play all orange and brown lettered notes with your right hand; all black with your left.

DECK THE HALLS

☛ Remember: B Flat is shown as ♭B.

C ♭B A G F GAF GA♭B

DECK THE HALLS WITH BOUGHS OF HOL...LY   FA LA LA

GAGFEF C♭BA GFGAF

LA LA LA LA LA LA   'TIS THE SEA...SON TO BE JOL...LY

GA♭BGAGFEF

FA LA LA LA LA LA LA LA LA

GA ♭B GA ♭BCG

DON WE NOW OUR GAY   AP...PAR...EL

A♭BCDEFEDC

FA LA LA LA LA LA LA LA LA

C ♭BA G F GAF

TROLL THE AN...CIENT YULE...TIDE CA...ROL

DDDDC♭BAGF

FA LA LA LA LA LA LA LA LA LA

Play all orange and brown lettered notes with your right hand; all black with your left.

JINGLE BELLS

☞ **Remember: B Flat is shown as ♭B.**

C A G F C   **C C C A G F D**

DASH...ING THROUGH THE SNOW   IN   A ONE HORSE OPEN   SLEIGH

D ♭B A G E   **C   C ♭B G A**

O'ER THE FIELDS WE GO   LAUGH...ING ALL THE WAY

C A G F C   **C A G F D**

BELLS ON BOB...TAILS RING   MAK...ING SPIR...ITS BRIGHT

D D ♭B A G C C C

WHAT FUN IT IS   TO   RIDE AND SING

C D   C ♭B G F

A   SLEIGH...ING SONG TO...NIGHT

CHORUS

A A A   A A A   A C F G A

JIN...GLE   BELLS, JIN...GLE BELLS   JIN...GLE ALL THE WAY,

Play all orange and brown lettered notes with your right hand; all black with your left.

14

JINGLE BELLS

☞ **Remember: B Flat is shown as ♭B.**

♭B ♭B ♭B ♭B ♭B A A

OH   WHAT   FUN   IT   IS   TO   RIDE

A A A G G A G C

IN   A   ONE HORSE O...PEN   SLEIGH

A A A   A A A   A C F G A

JIN...GLE BELLS, JIN...GLE BELLS   JIN...GLE ALL THE WAY.

♭B ♭B ♭B ♭B ♭B A A

OH   WHAT   FUN   IT   IS   TO   RIDE

A A C C ♭B G F

IN   A   ONE HORSE O...PEN SLEIGH.

Play all orange and brown lettered notes with your right hand; all black with your left.

I'VE BEEN WORKING ON THE RAILROAD

☛ Remember: B Flat is shown as ♭B.

F F C F C F G A F ♭B ♭B F

I'VE BEEN WORK...ING ON THE RAIL...ROAD   ALL   THE   LIVE

G A   F C F C F G A F

LONG DAY   I'VE BEEN WORKING ON THE RAIL...ROAD

A A A G G A G

JUST TO PASS THE TIME   A...WAY

G G G G A G F C

DON'T YOU HEAR THE WHIS...TLE BLOW...ING

♭B ♭B ♭B F F G G A

RISE   UP   SO EAR...LY   IN   THE   MORN

D E F E F D C F

DON'T YOU HEAR THE CAP...TAIN SHOUT...ING

A ♭B A G F

DI...NAH BLOW YOUR HORN...

Play all orange and brown lettered notes with your right hand; all black with your left.

16

I'VE BEEN WORKING ON THE RAILROAD

C C C   C F

DI...NAH, WON'T YOU BLOW

D D D   D G

DI...NAH WON'T YOU BLOW

E E E   E D E F G A

DI...   NAH WON'T YOU BLOW YOUR HOR...OR...ORN?

C C C   C F

DI...NAH WON'T YOU BLOW,

D D D D G

DI...NAH, WON'T YOU BLOW

E E E   E D E F

DI...NAH, WON'T YOU BLOW YOUR HORN?

2ND VERSE:

SOMEONE'S IN THE KITCHEN WITH DINAH
SOMEONE'S IN THE KITCHEN I KNOW
SOMEONE'S IN THE KITCHEN WITH DINAH
STRUMMIN' ON THE OLD BANJO
SINGING FEE FIE DIDDLE EE I O
FEE FIE FIDDLE EE I O O
FEE FIE FIDDLE EE I O O
STRUMMIN ON THE OLD BANJO

Play all orange and brown lettered notes with your right hand; all black with your left.

17

THE BLUE-TAIL FLY

☛ **Remember: B Flat is shown as ♭B.**

A ♭B A G F D D♭B D C F F F E

WHEN I WAS YOUNG I USE' TO WAIT ON MAS...TER AND HAND HIM

F G A ♭B A G G F D D ♭B

HIS PLATE, AND PASS THE PITCH...ER WHEN HE GOT DRY,

D C E G ♭B A F F

AN... BRUSH A...WAY THE BLUE...TAIL FLY.

CHORUS: ## C C F F F E G G

JIM...MIE CRACK CORN AN I DON'T CARE,

C C G G G F A A

JIM...MIE CRACK CORN AN' I DON'T CARE,

F F A A A♭B D D

JIM...MIE CRACK CORN AN I DON'T CARE,

D D C C ♭B G F

CAUSE MY MAS...TER'S GONE A...WAY.

Play all orange and brown lettered notes with your right hand; all black with your left.

POLLY WOLLY DOODLE

☞ **Remember: B Flat is shown as ♭B.**

F G A A F   **F G A A F**

OH, I   WENT DOWN SOUTH   FOR TO   SEE MY   SAL,

F F A A A A ♭B ♭B A A G

SING...ING POL...LY WOL...LY   DOD...DLE   ALL THE DAY.

E F G G E E G   G   E   E   E C C

OH MY SAL SHE IS A   SPUNK...Y   GAL,   SING...ING POL...LY

C C ♭B ♭B B G G F   F G A

WOL...LY DOO...   DLE ALL THE DAY   FARE THEE WELL,

F G A   F G A A ♭B A G   E

FARE THEE WELL,   FARE THEE WELL MY FAIR... Y FAY   FOR

E G G G G E E E E G G G G E E

I'M GOING TO LOU...SI...AN...A   FOR TO SEE MY SU...SY...AN...NA

G G C C C C ♭B ♭B B G G F

SING...ING POL...LY WOL...LY   DOO ...DLE ALL THE DAY.

Play all orange and brown lettered notes with your right hand; all black with your left.

ALL THROUGH THE NIGHT

☛ **Remember: B Flat is shown as ♭B.**

F E D F G F E C   D E

SLEEP MY LOVE AND PEACE ATTEND THEE   ALL THROUGH

E F   F E D F G F E C

THE NIGHT   GUARD...IAN AN...GELS GOD WILL LEND THEE,

D E E F

ALL THROUGH THE NIGHT

♭B A ♭B C D C ♭B A

SOFT THE DROW...SY HOURS ARE CREEP...ING,

♭B A G F A G F E

HILL   AND DALE IN SLUM...BER STEEP...ING

F E D F G F E C

LOVE A...LONE HIS WATCH IS KEEP...ING,

D E E F

ALL THROUGH THE NIGHT.

Play all orange and brown lettered notes with your right hand; all black with your left.

GOD REST YOU MERRY, GENTLEMEN

☞ Remember: B Flat is shown as ♭B.

D D A A G F E D   C D E

GOD REST YOU MER...RY GEN...TLE...MEN,   LET NOTH...ING

F G A   D D A A G F E D C

YOU DIS...MAY,   RE...MEM...BER CHRIST OUR SA...VI...OUR WAS

D E F   G A   A ♭B G A ♭B

BORN ON   CHRIST...MAS DAY,   TO SAVE US ALL FROM

C D A   G F D E F G

SA...TAN'S POWER,   WHEN WE WERE GONE A...STRAY.

CHORUS:

F G A ♭B A A G F E D   F   E

O...   TID...INGS   OF COM...   FORT AND JOY,   COM...FORT

D G   F G A ♭B C D A G F E D

AND JOY,   O   TID...   INGS OF COM... FORT AND JOY.

Play all orange and brown lettered notes with your right hand; all black with your left.

INTRODUCING THE F SHARP IN THE ORANGE SECTION

You have now learned about the B Flat and that all flats lie to the left of the white keys. Now it is time to learn about **F Sharps.**

A sharp is a note directly to the right of a white key, and for the F Sharp we are going to use in this book, it is the **black key** directly to the right of the Orange F.

Every note has a sharp, but we are going to again concentrate on one - the F Sharp. It will appear as:

#F

Double check your key board - Is the #F (F Sharp) on the black key between the Orange F and the Orange G?

Remember: The F Sharp will be shown as **#F.**

Review: All notes have sharps.
Sharps lie directly to the right of the white keys.
A sharp sign is #F for the one we are going to use.

DOWN IN THE VALLEY

☞ **Remember: F Sharp is shown as #F.**

D G A B G

DOWN IN   THE VAL...LEY,

B AG A

VAL...LEY   SO LOW,

D #F A D D

HANG YOUR HEAD O...VER,

C B A G

HEAR THE WIND BLOW.

D G A B G

HEAR THE WIND BLOW DEAR,

B A G A

HEAR THE WIND BLOW,

D #F A D D

HANG YOUR HEAD O...VER,

C B A G

HEAR THE WIND BLOW.

Play all orange and brown lettered notes with your right hand; all black with your left.

RED RIVER VALLEY

☛ **Remember: F Sharp is shown as #F.**

D G B B A G A G E G

FROM THIS VAL...LEY THEY SAY YOU ARE GO...ING

D G B G B D C B A

WE WILL MISS YOUR BRIGHT EYES AND SWEET SMILE,

D D B B A G A B D C

FOR THEY SAY YOU ARE TAK...ING THE SUN...SHINE

E D G A B A A G

THAT BRIGHT...ENS OUR PATH...WAY A...WHILE.

D G B B A G A G E G   D G

COME AND SIT BY MY SIDE IF YOU LOVE ME   DO NOT

B G B D C B A   D C B B A G

HAS...TEN TO BID ME A...DIEU   BUT RE...MEM...BER THE RED

A B D C E E D #F G A B A G

RIV...ER VAL...LEY AND THE GIRL THAT HAS LOVED YOU SO TRUE.

Play all orange and brown lettered notes with your right hand; all black with your left.

24

HARK THE HERALD ANGELS SING

☞ Remember: F Sharp is shown as #F.

D G G #F G B B A D D DD C B

HARK! THE HER...ALD AN...GELS SING, GLO...RY TO THE NEW

A B   **D G G #F G B B A**

BORN KING   PEACE ON EARTH, AND MER...CY MI...LD,

D A A #F #F E D   **D D D**

GOD AND SIN...NERS REC...ON....CILED   JOY...FUL ALL

G C B B A   **D D D G C B B A**

YE NA...TIONS RI...SE: JOIN THE TRI...UMPH OF THE SK...IES

E E E D C B C

WITH TH'AN...GEL...IC HOST PRO...CLAIM

A B C D G G A B   **E E E D**

CHRIST IS ... BORN IN BETH...LE...HEM.   HARK! THE HER...ALD

C B C   **A B C D G G A G**

AN...GELS SING,   GLO...RY TO THE NEW BORN KING.

Play all orange and brown lettered notes with your right hand; all black with your left.

THE STAR SPANGLED BANNER

☛ Remember: F Sharp is shown as #F.

G E C E G C   E D C   E #F G

O SAY   CAN YOU SEE   BY THE DAWN'S EAR...LY LIGHT

G G E D C B   A B C C G

WHAT SO PROUD...LY WE HAILED   AT THE TWI...LIGHT'S LAST

E C   G E C E G C

GLEAM...ING.   WHOSE BROAD STRIPES AND BRIGHT STARS,

E D C E #F G   G G E D

THRO' THE PER...I...LOUS FIGHT,   O'ER THE RAM...PARTS

C B   A B C C G E C

WE WATCHED,   WERE SO GAL...LANT...LY STREAM...ING.

E E E F G G F E D E F F

AND THE ROC...KETS RED GLARE, THE BOMBS BURST...ING IN AIR

F E D C B A B C E #F G

GAVE PROOF THRO' THE NIGHT   THAT OUR FLAG WAS STILL THERE

Play all orange and brown lettered notes with your right hand; all black with your left.

26

THE STAR SPANGLED BANNER

G C C C B A A A D F E D C C

OH SAY DOES THAT STAR SPANG...LED BAN... NER YET

B   **G G C D E F G**

WAVE   O'ER THE LAND   OF THE FREE

C D E F D C

AND THE HOME OF THE BRAVE.

Play all orange and brown lettered notes with your right hand; all black with your left.

BATTLE HYMN OF THE REPUBLIC

☞ **Remember: F Sharp is shown as ♯F.**

D D D D D C B D G A B B B A G

MINE EYES HAVE SEEN THE GLO...RY OF THE COM...ING OF THE LORD;

G ♯F E E E ♯F G ♯F G E D E

HE   IS TRAMP...LING OUT THE VIN...TAGE WHERE THE GRAPES OF

D B D   D D D D D C

WRATH ARE STORED;   HE HATH LOOS'D THE FATE...FUL

B D G A B B B A G

LIGHT...NING OF   HIS TER...RI...BLE SWIFT SWORD,

G A A G ♯F G

HIS TRUTH IS MARCH...ING ON.

CHORUS:

D C B D G A B G

GLO...RY, GLO...RY   HAL...LE...LU...JAH!

Play all orange and brown lettered notes with your right hand; all black with your left.

BATTLE HYMN OF THE REPUBLIC

E #FG#F G E D B

GLO...RY, GLO...RY   HAL...LE...LU...JAH!

D C B D G A B G

GLO...RY, GLO...RY HAL...LE...LU...JAH!

G A A G #F G

HIS TRUTH IS MARCH...ING ON.

Play all orange and brown lettered notes with your right hand; all black with your left.

WHEN JOHNNY COMES MARCHING HOME

☛ **Remember: F Sharp is shown as #F.**

E B E E E #F G #F G

WHEN JOHN...NY COMES MARCH...ING HOME   A...GAIN,

E D B D

HUR...RAH!   HUR...RAH!

E B E E E #F G #F G

WE'LL GIVE HIM A HEART...Y   WEL...COME THEN,

A B G B

HUR...RAH! HUR...RAH!

G B B B A G A A A

THE MEN WILL CHEER   THE BOYS WILL SHOUT,

#F G G #F E #F #F #F   G A

THE   LAD...IES THEY WILL ALL TURN OUT,   AND WE'LL

B A G   #F B E E E D E

ALL FEEL GAY   WHEN JOHN...NY COMES MARCH...ING HOME.

Play all orange and brown lettered notes with your right hand; all black with your left.

WE THREE KINGS OF ORIENT ARE

☞ Remember: F Sharp is shown as #F.

B A G E #F G #F E

WE   THREE   KINGS   OF   O... RI... ENT   ARE,

B A G E #F G #F E

BEAR...ING GIFTS, WE TRAV...ERSE   A...FAR.

G G A A B B DCB

FIELD AND FOUN...TAIN, MOOR AND 'MOUN....TAIN

A B A G #F E

FOL...LOW...ING YON...DER STAR.

Refrain: #FA G G G D   G E G

O... STAR   OF   WON...DER,   STAR OF NIGHT,

G G G D G E G   G G A B

STAR WITH ROY...AL BEAU...   BRIGHT,   WEST...WARD LEAD...ING

C B A B   G G G D G E G

STILL PRO...CEED...ING,   GUIDE US   TO THY   PER...FECT LIGHT.

Play all orange and brown lettered notes with your right hand; all black with your left.

GRAND OLD FLAG

☞ Remember: F Sharp is shown as #F.

C A F F F   **D CF G E F**

YOU'RE A GRAND OLD FLAG   YOU'RE A HIGH FLY...ING FLAG

DC FD C F D C E

AND FOR...EVER   IN PEACE MAY YOU WAVE

C C E F G C F G A

YOU'RE THE   EM...BLEM OF   THE LAND I   LOVE

F GA FGA F G C

THE HOME OF THE FREE AND THE BRA...VE.

C A F F F DC F G E F D

EV...ERY HEART BEATS TRUE FOR THE RED, WHITE AND BLUE   AND

C FDCFAG C F E F A

THERE'S NEV...ER A BURST OR BRAG   MAY OLD... A QUAIN...TANCE

G #F G C CD FD F G F

BE FOR...GOT   KEEP YOUR EYE ON THE GRAND OLD FLAG.

Play all orange and brown lettered notes with your right hand; all black with your left.

LITTLE BROWN JUG

☞ Remember: F Sharp is shown as #F.

D B D D D C E E

MY WIFE AND I   LIVED ALL A...LONE

E E #F #F E #F G A B

IN A   LIT...TLE   HUT WE CALL...ED OUR OWN.

D B D D DC E E

NOW SHE LOVED GIN AND   I   LOVED RUM

E #F #F E #F G D G

I   TELL YOU WHAT   WE'D LOTS OF FUN

B G D   C E E

CHORUS:

HA   HA   HA   YOU AND ME

#F #F #F E #F G A B   B G D

LIT...TLE BROWN JUG DON'T I LOVE THEE   HA HA HA

C E E   #F #F #F E #F A G G

YOU AND ME   LIT...TLE BROWN JUG DON'T I   LOVE THEE

Play all orange and brown lettered notes with your right hand; all black with your left.

33

FINGER PLACEMENT

Up until now, I have not worried you about where to place your fingers. I felt you had enough on your mind with just becoming familiar with your piano or organ. You have been getting ready for finger placement however, by playing all black-colored notes with your left hand and all orange and brown-colored notes with your right hand.

Now you are ready to move on and, in the songs that follow, I will suggest certain finger placement. Read carefully the below instructions!

LEFT HAND (used for black-lettered notes.)

RIGHT HAND (used for orange and brown-lettered notes.)

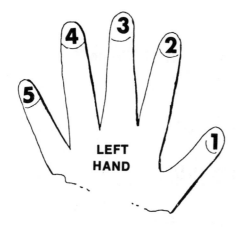
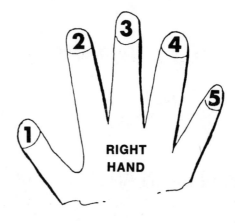

REMEMBER

*THE THUMB **FOR BOTH HANDS** IS NUMBERED #1.
*THE INDEX FINGER (next to thumb) IS #2 **ON BOTH HANDS**.
*THE NUMBERING **ON BOTH HANDS** CONTINUES 3, 4, 5 . . . as above picture.
*HAND SIZES WILL VARY AND, IF SOMETHING FEELS TERRIBLY UNCOMFORTABLE, AFTER TRYING IT SEVERAL TIMES, FEEL FREE TO CHANGE IT TO FINGERING YOU PREFER. CHILDREN UNDER NINE YEARS OF AGE WILL OFTEN HAVE DIFFICULTY WITH FINGERING, DUE TO THEIR SMALL HANDS. IF THIS HAPPENS, LET THEM USE THE FINGERS THEY WISH TO PLAY THE SONGS.

EXAMPLES OF FINGERING IN THE PAGES THAT FOLLOW:

G

(MEANS THE NOTE YOU WILL BE PLAYING)

3 (MEANS THE FINGER YOU WILL USE)

Because G is a black-lettered note, you will play it with your left hand using #3 finger.

POP GOES THE WEASEL

C C D D E G E C
1 1 2 2 3 5 3 1

ALL A...ROUND THE COB...BL...ER'S BENCH

G C C D D E C
3 1 1 2 2 3 1

THE MON...KEY CHASE...D THE WEA...SEL

G C C D D E G E C
3 1 1 2 2 3 5 3 1

THE MON...KEY THOUGHT T'WAS ALL   IN FUN

A D F E C
5 2 4 3 1

POP GOES THE WEA...SEL.

Play all orange and brown lettered notes with your right hand; all black with your left.

SHE'LL BE COMIN' ROUND THE MOUNTAIN WHEN SHE COMES

☞ Remember: B Flat is shown as ♭B.

C **D** **F** **F** **F** **F** **D** **C** **A** **C** **F**
1   2   4   4   4   4   2   1   2   1   4

SHE'LL BE COM...IN' ROUND THE MOUN...TAIN WHEN SHE COMES.

F **G** **A** **A** **A** **A** **C** **A** **G** **F** **G**
1   2   3   3   3   3   5   3   2   1   2

SHE'LL BE COM...IN ROUND THE MOUN...TAIN WHEN SHE COMES.

C **♭B** **A** **A** **A** **A** **G** **F**
5   4   3   3   3   3   2   1

SHE'LL BE COM...IN ROUND THE MOUN...TAIN,

F **F** **D** **D** **D** **D** **G** **F**
1   1   2   2   2   2   5   4

SHE'LL BE COM...IN ROUND THE MOUN...TAIN

E **D** **C** **C** **C** **C** **A** **G**
3   2   1   1   1   1   5   4

SHE'LL BE COM...IN' ROUND THE MOUN...TAIN

D **E** **F**
1   2   3

WHEN SHE COMES.

Play all orange and brown lettered notes with your right hand; all black with your left.

36

GOOD NIGHT LADIES

E C G C
3 1 3 1
GOOD NIGHT LA...DIES

E C D D
3 1 2 2
GOOD NIGHT LA...DIES

E C F F
3 1 4 4
GOOD NIGHT LA....DIES

F E E D D C
4 3 3 2 2 1
WE HATE TO SEE YOU GO

E D C D E E E
3 2 1 2 3 3 3
MER...RI...LY   WE ROLL A...LONG,

D D D   E G G
2 2 2   3 5 5
ROLL A...LONG,   ROLL A...LONG

E D C D E E E
3 2 1 2 3 3 3
MER...RI....LY WE ROLL   A...LONG

D D E D C
2 2 3 2 1
O...ER THE DEEP BLUE SEA.

Play all orange and brown lettered notes with your right hand; all black with your left.

TEN LITTLE INDIANS

C C C C C C E G G E D C
1 1 1 1 1 1 3 5 5 3 2 1

ONE LIT...TLE, TWO LIT...TLE, THREE LIT...TLE IN...DI...ANS,

D D D D D D B D D B A G
2 2 2 2 2 2 1 2 2 1 2 3

FOUR LIT...TLE FIVE LIT...TLE SIX LIT...TLE, IN...DI...ANS,

C C C C C C E G G E D C
1 1 1 1 1 1 3 5 5 3 2 1

SEVEN LIT...TLE   EIGHT LIT...TLE, NINE LIT...TLE IN...DI...ANS,

G F F E E D C
5 4 4 3 3 2 1

TEN LIT...TLE IN...DI...AN BOYS

2nd Verse:

Ten little, nine little, eight little Indians,
Seven little, six little, five little Indians,
Four little, three little, two little Indians,
One little, Indian boy.

Play all orange and brown lettered notes with your right hand; all black with your left.

HERE COMES THE BRIDE

G C C C
3 1 1 1
HERE COMES THE BRIDE

G D B C
3 2 1 1
BIG, FAT AND WIDE

G C F F E
3 1 4 4 3
HERE COMES THE GRO....OM

D C C B C D
2 1 1 1 1 2
SKIN...NY   AS A BROOM

G C C C
3 1 1 1
HERE COMES THE BRIDE,

G D B C
3 2 1 2
BIG FAT AND WIDE

G C E G E C
3 1 3 5 3 1
HERE COMES THE GRO...OM

A A D E C
2 2 2 3 1
SKIN...NY   AS A BROOM.

Play all orange and brown lettered notes with your right hand; all black with your left.

CHORDS
(Recommended for Ages 9 or Older)

Congratulations! If you have reached this far and can play all of the songs, you have done very well. I know some of you are ready to go one step further and play the piano with both hands at a time. I will not go into Chords in detail, but I will give you three chords that you will be able to play with most melodies.

A Chord is usually a group of 3 notes played together to give one sound. The Chord will be played with the left hand.

The Melody will be notes played in the orange and brown-lettered areas and will always be played with the right hand. This practice of playing chords with the left hand and the melody with the right is not the case in all music but will be followed without exception in this book.

INTRODUCING THE C CHORD

The C Chord we will be using is in the black section and is:

The Black C played with the No. 5 finger of the left hand,
The Black E played with the No. 3 finger of the left hand, and
The Black G played with the No. 1 finger of the left hand.

Remember, These Notes Are Played All Together!

Play the C Chord (CEG in the black section) with your left hand hitting all the notes at once. At the same time you are playing the chord, hit the Orange C with the No. 1 finger of your right hand.

Play the C Chord (CEG in the black section) with your left hand hitting all the notes at once, and at the same time, hit the Orange E with the No. 3 finger of your right hand.

Play the C Chord (CEG in the black section) with your left hand hitting all the notes at once, and, at the same time, hit the Orange G with the No. 5 finger of your right hand. (This may also be done with the Brown C, Brown E and Brown G one at a time.)

Remember: You are hitting the C Chord and the Orange note all at the same time. (We are using an Orange note as an example here, but you may be playing a brown note with a chord in some of the songs.)

In the songs which will follow using chords, you play the chord only above the note indicated. For example, it will be shown this way:

C   (Means the chord you will hit using the left hand.)

E   (Means the note you will play using the right hand.)

3   (Means the finger on the right hand you will use.)

USING C CHORD
MARY HAD A LITTLE LAMB

Remember: All Chords Are Played With The Left Hand.

C   **C**   **C**

E D C D E E E

3 2 1 2 3 3 3

MA....RY HAD A LIT....TLE LAMB,

         C   **C**

D D D E G G

2 2 2 3 5 5

LIT....TLE LAMB, LIT....TLE LAMB.

C   **C**   **C**

E D C D E E E

3 2 1 2 3 3 3

MA....RY HAD A LIT....TLE LAMB,

               C

E D D E D C

3 2 2 3 2 1

ITS FLEECE WAS WHITE AS SNOW.

Play all orange and brown lettered notes with your right hand; all black with your left.

INTRODUCING THE G CHORD

The next chord we will study is the G Chord. It has two Black-lettered notes and one orange-lettered note and is played as follows:

The Black G played with the No. 5 finger of the left hand,
The Black B played with the No. 3 finger of the left hand, and
The Orange D played with the No. 1 finger of the left hand.

Remember These 3 Notes Are Played All Together!

To Practice the G Chord:

Play the G Chord (GBD) with your left hand hitting all the notes at once. At the same time you are playing the chord, hit the Orange G with the No. 1 finger of the right hand.

Play the G Chord (GBD) with your left hand hitting all the notes at once. At the same time you are playing the chord hit the Orange B with the No. 3 finger of the right hand.

Play the G Chord (GBD) with the left hand hitting all the notes at once, and at the same time hit the Brown D with the No. 5 finger of the right hand.

The G Chord (GBD) usually sounds all right with most notes that are G or B in the Orange Section and D, G or B in the Brown Section.

Remember: You are hitting the G Chord with the left hand at the same time you are hitting an Orange note or a Brown note with the right hand.

USING G CHORD
ALOUETTE

Remember: All Chords Are Played With The Left Hand.

G			**G**				**G**			
G	A	B	B	A	G		A	B	G	D
3	4	5	5	4	3		4	5	3	1
A	LOU	ET	TE, GEN...TLE				A...LOU...ET...TE			

G			**G**					**G**
G	A	B	B		A	G	A	B	G
3	4	5	5		4	3	4	5	3
A	LOU	ET	TE		JE	TE	PLU	ME	RAI

G				**G**	**G**	
G	G	G	B	D	D	D
1	1	1	3	5	5	5
JE	TE	PLU	ME	RAI	LA TETE	

				G		**G**						
D	E	D	C	B	A	G		D	D	D	D	D	D
4	5	4	3	2	1	2		5	5	5	1	1	1
JE	TE PLU	ME		RAI	LA TETE			ET LA TETE			ET LA TETE		

D
5

OH! (Repeat lines 1 and 2 for refrain)

Play all orange and brown lettered notes with your right hand; all black with your left.

43

INTRODUCING THE F CHORD

The last chord we will study and use is the F Chord. It is played as follows:

The Black F played with the No. 5 finger of the left hand,
The Black A played with the No. 3 finger of the left hand, and
The Orange C played with the No. 1 finger of the left hand.

To Practice the F Chord:

Play the F Chord (FAC) with your left hand hitting all the notes at the same time.

Play the F Chord (FAC) with your left hand and at the same time, hit the Orange F with the No. 1 finger of the right hand.

Play the F Chord (FAC) with your left hand and at the same time, hit the Orange A with the No. 3 finger of the right hand.

Play the F Chord (FAC) with your left hand and at the same time hit the Brown C with the No. 5 finger of the right hand.

Then try the F Chord with the Brown F with the No. 1 finger of the right hand. Try also the F Chord with the Brown A. Use the No. 3 finger of the right hand.

Remember: You play the three notes of the chord all at the same time while you are hitting a note in the Orange or Brown section.

LET'S REVIEW CHORDS

The **C Chord** is **CEG** played with the **left** hand.

The **G Chord** is **GBD** played with the **left** hand.

The **F Chord** is **FAC** played with the **left** hand.

Remember—all 3 notes in a chord are played at the same time!

Remember: All Chords Are Played With The Left Hand.

B Flat is Shown As ♭B.
F Sharp Is Shown As ♯F.

USING F CHORD
OLD McDONALD HAD A FARM

F   F   F

F F F C D D C   **A A G G F**

4 4 4 1 2 2 1   5 5 4 4 3

OLD Mc...DON...ALD HAD A FARM   E.... I... E... I.... 0

F   F   F

C F F F C D D C A A G G F

1 4 4 4 1 2 2 1 5 5 4 4 3

AND ON THIS FARM HE HAD SOME CHICKS E... I... E... I.... 0

F   F   F

C C F F F C C F F F

1 1 4 4 4 1 1 4 4 4

WITH A CHICK CHICK HERE AND A CHICK CHICK THERE

F   F   F   F

F F F F F F F F F F F F

4 4 4 4 4 4 4 4 4 4 4 4

HERE A CHICK THERE A CHICK EV....ERY....WHERE A CHICK CHICK

F   F   F

F F F C D D C   **A A G G F**

4 4 4 1 2 2 1   5 5 4 4 3

OLD Mc...DON...ALD HAD A FARM   E... I... E.... I.... 0

Remember: All Chords Are Played With The Left Hand.

MORE SONGS WITH CHORDS
TWINKLE TWINKLE LITTLE STAR

Remember: All Chords Are Played With The Left Hand.

C   **F**

C C G G A A G

1   1   4   4   5   5   4

TWIN...KLE TWIN...KLE LIT...TLE STAR

F   **C**

F F E E D D C

4   4   3   3   2   2   1

HOW I WON...DER WHERE YOU ARE

C   **F**

G G F F E E D

5   5   4   4   3   3   2

UP   A...BOVE THE SKY SO HIGH.

         G

G G F F E E D

5   5   4   4   3   3   2

LIKE   A   DIA....MOND IN THE SKY

C   **F**

C C G G A A G

1   1   4   4   5   5   4

TWIN...KLE TWIN...KLE LIT...TLE STAR,

F   **C**

F F E E D G C

4   4   3   3   2   5   1

HOW I WON...DER WHERE YOU ARE.

46

KOOKABURRA

Remember: All Chords Are Played With The Left Hand.

C   **F**   **C**

G G G G A A A G E G E

4 4 4 4 5 5 5 4 2 4 2

KOO...KA...BUR...RA SITS   IN THE OLD GUM TR...EE.

                                        C

E E E E F F F E C E C

2 2 2 2 3 3 3 2 1 2 1

MER...RY MER...RY KING OF THE BUSH IS HE

           F

C A B C A

5 3 4 5 3

LAUGH KOO...KA...BUR...RA,

C

G E F G F

2 1 2 3 2

LAUGH KOO...KA...BUR...RA

         C

E C C C C

2 1 1 1 1

GAY YOUR LIFE MUST BE.

Play all orange and brown lettered notes with your right hand; all black with your left.

HICKORY DICKORY DOCK

Remember: All Chords Are Played With The Left Hand.

C **G** **C**
E F G F E D E
3 4 5 4 3 2 3
HIC...KOR...Y   DIC...KOR....Y DOCK

C **G** **C**
E E G F D E
3 3 5 4 2 3
THE MOUSE RAN UP THE CLOCK

C **C**
E E E G
3 3 3 5
THE CLOCK STRUCK ONE

F **F**
G F F A
5 4 4 5
THE MOUSE RAN DOWN

C **G** **C**
G A G F E D C
4 5 4 3 2 1 2
HIC...KOR...Y   DIC...KOR...Y DOCK.

Play all orange and brown lettered notes with your right hand; all black with your left.

48

LONDON BRIDGE

C C C C

G A G F E F G

4 5 4 3 2 3 4

LON...DON BRIDGE IS FALL...ING DOWN

F C C

D E F **E F G**

1 2 3 2 3 4

FALL...ING DOWN, FALL...ING DOWN.

C C

G A G F E F G

4 5 4 3 2 3 4

LON...DON BRIDGE IS FALL...ING DOWN

C

D G E C

2 5 3 1

MY FAIR LA....DY.

OLD FOLKS AT HOME

Now try your hands at finger placement.

C   **C**   **F**

E D C **E D** C   **C** A C

WAY DOWN UP...ON THE SWAN...EE RIV...ER,

C   **C**

G E C **D**   **E**   **D** C **E** D

FAR, FAR A...WAY   THERE'S WHERE MY HEART IS

C   **F**   **C**

C **C** A C   **G** E C **D**

TURN...ING EV...ER: THERE'S WHERE THE OLD

                  C   **C**

D C   **E D** C **E** D C

FOLKS STAY   ALL UP AND DOWN THE WHOLE

   F   **C**

C A **C**   **G** E C **D**

CRE...A...TION   SAD...LY I ROAM,

Remember: All Chords Are Played With The Left Hand.

50

OLD FOLKS AT HOME

C   **C**   **F**

E D C E D C C A C

STILL LONG...ING FOR THE OLD PLAN...TA...TION,

C   **C**

G E C D D D C

AND FOR THE OLD FOLKS AT HOME.

CHORUS: **G**   **G C**

B C D G G A G C

ALL THE WORLD IS SAD AND DREAR...Y

F   **C**   **G**   **C**

C A F A G E D C E D C

EVERY...WHERE I ROAM, O DAR...KIES, HOW MY HEART

F   **C**   **C**

C A C G E C D D D C

GROWS WEARY, FAR FROM THE OLD FOLKS AT HOME.

THREE BLIND MICE

Remember: All Chords Are Played With The Left Hand.

C
E D C

C
E D C

THREE BLIND MICE

THREE BLIND MICE

F
G F F E

F
G F F E

SEE HOW THEY RUN

SEE HOW THEY RUN

C
G C C B A B C G G

G

THEY ALL RUN AF...TER THE   FAR...MER'S WIFE

C
G C C B A B C G G

G

WHO CUT OFF THEIR TAILS WITH A   CAR...VING KNIFE

C
G G C C B A B C G G G

DID   YOU EV...ER SEE SUCH A SIGHT IN YOUR LIFE

C
F E

C
D C

AS THREE BLIND MICE.

Play all orange and brown lettered notes with your right hand; all black with your left.

52

ON TOP OF OLD SMOKY

Remember: All Chords Are Played With The Left Hand.

C   F   F

C C E G C A A F G A G

ON TOP OF OLD SMOK...Y   ALL COV....ERED WITH SNOW

C   F

C C E G G D E F E D C

I LOST MY TRUE LOV...ER   A COURT...IN TOO SLOW

2nd Verse:
A Courtins A Pleasure
A Partin' Is Grief
A False Hearted Lover
Is Worse Than A Thief

3rd Verse:
A Thief He Will Rob You
And Take What You Have
But A False Hearted Lover
Will Lead You To The Grave

4th Verse:
They'll Hug You and Kiss You
And Tell You More Lies
Than The Leaves On A Willow
Or The Stars In The Skies

5th Verse:
My Sad Heart Is Aching
I'm Weary Today
My Lover Has Left Me
I'm Feelin' This Way

6th Verse:
It's rainin', It's Pourin'
The Moon Gives No Light
My Horse He Won't Travel
This Dark Lonesome Night.

7th Verse:
I'm Goin' Away, Dear
I'll Write You My Mind
My Mind Is To Marry
And To Leave You Behind.

8th Verse:
Come All You Young People
And Listen To Me
Don't Place Your Affection
On A Green Willow Tree

9th Verse:
The Leaves They Will Wither
The Roots They Will Die
You Will Be Forsaken
And Never Know Why.

10th Verse:
(Repeat Verse 1)

Play all orange and brown lettered notes with your right hand; all black with your left.

CHANGING OVER TO READING OF MUSIC
(Suggested for Ages 9 and Over)

There will be some of you who will want to stop your **Piano Fun** right here and that is fine. Continue playing the tunes in Book One and Book Two and enjoying yourself. There will be others of you who will want to go on and learn to read music by the notes rather than by the letter. This is no simple task and it will require memorizing where the notes are as well as basic rules. This chapter is to be used **as a guide** for you, as there are many exceptions in music, many of which we cannot cover in Book Two.

Below you will find what is called "The Great Musical Staff." It shows the location of the color-coded notes you have learned. Note Orange C between the 2 sets of lines - this "C" is always called "Middle C" and always has a line through the middle of it.

MEMORIZE THE FOLLOWING

TREBLE OR G CLEF

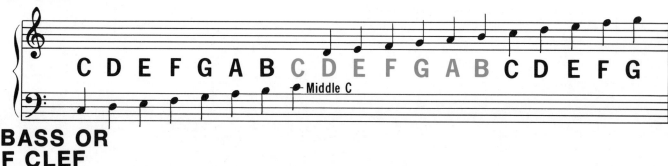

BASS OR F CLEF

(The above notes are those notes used in Piano Fun One and Two)

1. All orange and brown-lettered notes that you have previously learned are in the area called "The Treble Clef" or sometimes referred to as "The G Clef."

2. All black-lettered notes you've learned about are in the "Bass Clef" or sometimes referred to as the "F Clef."

3. A note always gets its name from the line or space on which it sits. It will be helpful if you can memorize these notes by their position on the line or space.

THE KEY SIGNATURE

At the beginning of every song you will ever play you will find a **Key Signature** 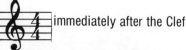 immediately after the Clef sign. The key signature will have one of three possible contents.

1. Sharps (♯ ♯) — You may find 1 or 2 or as many as 7.

2. Flats (♭ ♭) — You may find 1 or 2 or as many as 7.

3. Nothing At All — which identifies the C major scale which has no sharps or flats.

The sharp(s) or flat(s) are on the space(s) or line(s) of the notes that are to be played as sharps or flats. throughout the song.

RHYTHM

Also at the beginning of every song you will ever play, you will find two numbers that look like a fraction. This is called the **Time Signature.** (See drawing below!)

Time Signature

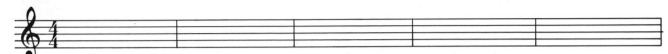

BAR LINE   BAR LINE   BAR LINE

The **top number** of the Time Signature tells you how many beats there are to a measure.

The **bottom number** in the Time Signature tells you what kind of a note receives 1 beat.

A Measure is the distance from 1 bar line to the next. (See above drawing.)

The Time Signature shown above indicates by the top number (4) that there are four (4) beats to the measure and the bottom number tells you that a quarter note receives one beat.

NOTES AND RESTS

Every beat in each song is shown by either a note or a rest. There are five kinds of each and are shown below. LEARN THEM BY MEMORY!

5 DIFFERENT NOTES IN MUSIC

| WHOLE | HALF | QUARTER | EIGHTH | SIXTEENTH |

○   **WHOLE NOTE**—represented in bottom of Time Signature by the No. 1

♩   **HALF NOTE**—represented in bottom of Time Signature by the No. 2

♩   **QUARTER (OR FOURTH) NOTE**—represented in bottom of Time Signature by the No. 4

♪   **EIGHTH NOTE**—represented in bottom of Time Signature by the No. 8

♪   **SIXTEENTH NOTE**—represented in bottom of time signature by the No. 16

These notes are represented by the bottom number in the Time Signature which tells what kind of note receives one beat.

DOTTED NOTES:

When a dot comes after a note, it adds one-half the value of the note that precedes it.

EXAMPLES:

𝅗𝅥. = 𝅗𝅥 (half note) + ♩ (quarter note)   The quarter note is half of the half note.

♪. = ♪ (one-eighth note) + 𝅘𝅥𝅯   One sixteenth is half of the eighth note.

RESTS

Every beat in each song is shown by either a note or a rest. There are five rests as there are five notes. MEMORIZE THEM!

| WHOLE | HALF | QUARTER | EIGHTH | SIXTEENTH |

Hangs From Line   **Sits On Line**

DOTTED RESTS

When a dot comes after a rest it <u>adds</u> one-half the value of the rest that precedes it.

EXAMPLE:

▬. = ▬ + ❧   A quarter rest is one-half of the half rest.

56

READING SONGS

Now that you have learned your notes, let's see if you can play the following tunes. They are written just as the song would be, except letters are being used too.

CLEMENTINE

Remember to make "B" a Flat.

F F F C A A A F F A C C B A G G A

B B A G A F F A G C E G F F F

F C A A A F F A C C B A G G A

B B A G A F F A G C E G F

Another tune that you might enjoy playing is Frere Jacques. Again, the letters are below. Have fun!

FRERE JACQUES

TRY ANOTHER SONG
(This time With Only Notes!)

She'll Be Comin' Round The Mountain

NAME THE TUNE

All of the below tunes are in **Piano Fun Book One** or **Piano Fun Book Two**. Can you name them? (Answers on next page.)

1.

1. _____

2.

2. _____

3.

3. _____

NAME THE TUNE (CONTINUED)

4.

4. _____

5. (Remember F is Sharp)

5. _____

OTHER BOOKS BY NANCY POFFENBERGER

INSTANT PIANO FUN – BOOK 1

The first in her series which begins for any child who knows ABC's as well as the colors black, orange and brown. Includes large ABC letters as well as color-coded stickers.

INSTANT ORGAN FUN FOR CHRISTMAS

Features 18 fun Christmas songs for any keyboard. Includes Up On The Housetop, It's A Small World, Let It Snow! Let It Snow! Let It Snow!

INSTANT FUN WITH SACRED SONGS

Features 21 songs – Amazing Grace, KumBaYa, The Church In The Wildwood, He's Got The Whole World In His Hand.

FUN WITH BELLS AND XYLOPHONES

Features 14 songs for 3-5 year olds...for any 8 note bells or xylophone...ABC Music...Picture Titles

RECORDER FUN BOOK ONE

A recorder book all done in ABC's...written for Montesorri through grade 3 as well as Special Classes (excellent simplification.).

RECORDER FUN BOOK TWO

(co-author – Rosemary Chaney Bane)
A Recorder book written for grades 3-6...includes a pull-out fingering chart, all done in musical notation...a perfect book for the elementary grades.

INSTANT PIANO FUN FOR CHRISTMAS

Features 18 fun Christmas songs for any keyboard. Includes Up On The Housetop, It's A Small World, Let It Snow! Let It Snow! Let It Snow!

Please contact your local store for these books. If unable to buy them please write:

The Fun Publishing Co.
2121 Alpine Drive
Cincinnati, Ohio 45206

To reorder Piano or Organ tabs, please send $3.95 for each set, along with Your Name, Address and Zip Code:

The Fun Publishing Co.
2121 Alpine Drive
Cincinnati, Ohio 45206

They will be mailed postage paid to address given.